WHO IS THE MAN CALLED

FINAS C. BLACK SR

(In the Midwest)

To *Francis*

I am so love by my Family
I am the great, great, great
Person I can be
I Know Faith hope,

Finas C Black Sr

7-5-2024

Dedication

I dedicate this book to my father whom I did not know. He was not in my life. To my stepfather who married my mother years later. To my wife, very loving, is gone but not missing. In Memory: This book is in memory of all family members and friends. Thanks: I want to thank all my friends and relatives for encouraging me to write a book.

My friends say Be Safe and Be Careful. I call myself Finas Black of the Midwest because I live in the Midwest. I like black cars and because I am a Black man, my last name is Black so it's black on black in black. On the front cover is a 2023 Honda Pilot EX L. It has about everything you want in a car. Leather seat, seven passenger V6 motor, 1 O speed automatic transmission, and many more Items.

Experience the love: All the love that was part of my life as I came into the world.

Acknowledgement

Grandfather, grandmother, uncle, aunts, cousin, my mother, my step daddy, my sister, my brothers, Mother in law, father in law, all my friends. All above people help to be my very best.

Table of Contents

Chapter 1

Born a son of a father and mother in the spring of 1945. I am also a grandson, nephew, and cousin. Who named me Finas? My grandmother named me Finas. Her son, Finas, went to the army in World War li. She did not want to lose her son in the war. He did not die in the war; he returned home and lived a long life. I was born in a small town in Missouri, about 1 OO miles south of St. Louis. I was born at home with a midwife. People called my uncle Big Finas and me Little Finas, in a small town in Illinois. Later, I would visit him and his family after I grew up. He worked at a grocery store.

I would visit him at the grocery store. The people would call for him over the speaker. My Uncle and I would come to the counter at the same time. They would ask for my uncle. I would say yes. They would respond, "Not you, him." My uncle would say his name is Finas too. We had a lot of fun doing this when we were together. I recall the greatest memory of 1945 was my coming into the world. In 1946, my mother kept me from being bitten by a rattlesnake. She killed the snake. The snake was about three feet long. My mother saved the dead snake to show my father that she had killed the snake, but the pigs got out of the pig pen and ate the snake. This showed me love and protection from my mother at a young age.

In 194 7, I was growing and learning. My mother and father had a baby girl. I became a big brother in the summer of 1947. I had a sister to play with. In 1948, I was still growing and learning. I had a baby sister to play with. She was about one year old. We had toys to play with. In 1949, what I thought was a birthmark on my foot was a burn mark from when I tried to climb on the stove, and a pot of beans fell on my foot. I was taken to the hospital and treated. My mother told me this story years later. My mother and father had a son in the late spring of 1949. Now I am a big brother to a brother and sister. In 1950, I started kindergarten. I learned my colors, numbers, and alphabet. In 1951, in late summer, I started first grade.

I learned to read and write while still growing and learning. My mother showed me how to work around the house, such as taking out the trash, doing laundry, and other household chores. In 1951, in the winter, my parents welcomed a baby boy. In 1952, I started second grade and began receiving homework. This is also the year my uncle died. I was standing too close to the gravesite. I was bending over too far and nearly fell in. My cousin grabbed me and said you are standing too close and will fall in—an example of how love and protection have always surrounded me; the year 1953 started in third grade. I began receiving more household chores such as bringing in wood, water from the faucet from outside, and picking up coal from the railroad yard in my little red wagon. The toilet was outside, and toilet paper was a catalog. My dad and I used to sit on the front porch and name the cars. I would walk around and look at the names of cars, so when my dad would ask me the names of the cars. I would know the names.

He thought I was so smart. Early on, I learned about sex from my older cousins; they were about ten to fifteen years older than me. They had books with naked women inside and posing in different positions. They also bragged about the sexual relations they had with their girlfriends. They would take me with them when they went to visit their girlfriends and told me not to tell anyone that they were having sex with their girlfriends. In 1954, another addition to the family was a baby girl. Late summer of 1955, we moved from a little town in Illinois to Omaha, NE.

Chapter 2

We moved to Omaha because my stepfather, whom I acknowledge as the only father in my life, had a few sisters who lived there. The drive to Omaha, NE, was about 9 hours. We lived with my aunt for about four months. I started a private school in 1955. In 1956we moved to a four-bedroom apartment with a washer machine and dryer hook up. We had a two-story apartment, a major upgrade from our humble beginnings—running water, in-house toilets, and my bedroom. I was so excited! My dad found a job working for the city as a sanitation worker. While living in this new apartment complex, I had to learn how to fight.

I had to learn how to fight because I was the new kid on the block. Four boys would try to fight me at once. One day, while they were in the process of hitting me. My mother yelled, take off your belt and hit them with your belt buckle. So as she stated and so I did. I began swinging my belt and hit a few of the kids. I started carrying a stick with me so I would swing it anytime they tried to run up on me. Once I caught them one on one, I would get them. There was a new game called Knock the Chip off The Shoulder.

When the kids tried to play the game with me, I would knock them out. They did not like that. My father was a boxer in the service. He taught me how to box and protect myself. Boxing was not the only sport that spiked my interest. There was also basketball. I learned how to play and was on the grade school team. I thought I was good until ninth grade when I was a bench warmer. In 1956, my mother and I became Catholics. My father was already catholic. I also became an altar boy during mass. I also asked if I could have my last name changed to Black. My mother and father began to work on that.

As soon as the last name was changed. I went to school the next day and told every one of my name change. To my surprise, becoming a Catholic, we attended mass five days a week in school; the Catholic Church has mass seven days a week. We have choirs that sing, we have Holy Communion every day, and we learned all the different things about the bible in grade school and high school. We had to learn about the bible every day. In 1957, my dad's friend had a garden in Iowa; he told my dad that he needed someone to work the garden as his friend was getting older. My dad would grow green beans, corn, cabbage, peppers, tomatoes, carrots, and small cantaloupes.

I would help him once I got out of school. One day after I helped my father tend to his garden, I grabbed a tomato while walking home, eating tomato with salt and pepper. The neighborhood kids came up to me and tried to take my tomato. I threw the salt and pepper from my hand into his eyes, and he ran off. In 1958, I had a bad experience in a taxi cab. The taxi company did not have very good cars. My mother called a cab for a morning pick-up. The cab driver took us to a location so my siblings and I could get our shots for school. Once we finished, a different cab driver picked us up. The taxi cab's front door was dented and hard to open up.

There was also no air conditioning and an awful smell in the cab. We rolled down the windows to air out the cab. I sat in the front seat. We were about two miles from the apartment building; the driver was driving fast and almost hit a pedestrian. The front door flew open, and I had to hold the door close until we made it home. Once we got home, my mother paid the driver and said I would never take a cab again. I told her I will drive you everywhere when I get a car. I was a boy scout in seventh and eighth grade.

Chapter 3

In the year 1959, we moved into a five-bedroom house. This house was equipped with a living room, dining room, two bathrooms, a fenced-in backyard, a basement, and a detached garage. We rented a moving truck, and all my siblings and I helped move our belongings into the house. The house had no stove or refrigerator; my parents had to buy one. I graduated in eighth grade. The school provided caps and gowns. At 14, I asked if my mother could sign off for me to begin working. My first job was at a grocery store. I was a sacker and helped customers carry their groceries to the car. I would receive tips for helping customers load their groceries into their cars.

During the summer, I would work all week and only have Saturdays off. On the Saturday I had off, my cousin suggested we go to a football game. I agreed. When it was time to get ready to go, they all changed their mind. I still wanted to go. So I went. I caught the bus with the assistance of the bus drivers because the location was far. I enjoyed the game. I returned to my cousin's house, and my parents were waiting for me. My cousins did not let my parents know I had left for the game. My parents were shocked that I made it to the game by myself. My mother hugged me and said to use a pay phone to call and let me know. She told me I would never be lost because I could navigate the city alone. My summer job allowed me to purchase a bicycle. I put ten dollars down toward the lay-a-way purchase of my bike. The bike total was twenty-five dollars. I was able to get the bike out of layaway a week later. I put mud flaps on the front and back fenders and purchased a new seat and basket in the front.

I carried a newspaper and groceries in my basket. I had a newspaper route for about two months. I had about fifty customers. I delivered papers, too; Sunday was the heaviest route I had. I no longer worked once the summer ended, and I went to high school. I began playing freshman basketball, which was not as good as I thought. I was about 6 feet tall in the ninth grade. I played varsity in my junior and senior years. Insert basketball picture here in the summer of 1959; I began to have nosebleeds a couple of times a day. I would blow my nose, and a blood clot would come out. I did not tell my mother until I woke up with blood all over me one morning. She put a cold towel over my head.

The following day I woke up to another bloody mess. This time my mother and father took me to a catholic hospital. The doctor observed me and said I needed to be admitted immediately for surgery. My tonsils and adenoids needed to be removed. The surgery went well. I prayed and asked for help to be alright. I had to stay in the hospital for a total of three days. A year later, I began to read. Reading became one of my favorite hobbies. The different genres I was interested in were romantic, fiction, cooking, sewing, trucking, carpenter work, and painting. I enjoyed reading because it helped me learn, and I could converse with anyone.

Chapter 4

My cousin taught me how to drive a Ford. I began working again in the summer of 1961. This job was at a car wash; I washed and sanded cars down for painting. This job also increased my driving skills, as I had to drive the cars to their designated parking spaces. One day I was walking and saw a used car lot down the street from my job. I began looking at the cars, and the car that piqued my interest was a stick shift. I went to talk to the salesman at the car lot. He said the car was a 1952 Plymouth, two-door. The car cost $25. I asked the salesman to hold the car until I got paid.

He required that I put in a deposit of $10. I later asked my father if he could sign for me to get this vehicle because I was underage, and he said no. Then later stated if the car were brand new, he would sign for me. I asked one of my coworkers, whom I became friends with if he could cosign for me, and he said yes.

I paid the remaining balance for the car. The car was in bad shape, but I needed something to practice. There was brick holding up the front seat, and smoke was coming out of the tailpipe; when I hit a bump in the road, the muffler would fall off. I would have to stop, pick it up, and place it back on; I drove the car home and practiced in the alleys until I got the license plate for the car.

My car burned more oil than gas. I used to put five quarts of oil in my car every day. The car lasted about eight months. Gas was twenty cents a gallon at that time.

In my senior year, 1962, my basketball coach asked if any male students wanted to box. I said yes, and I signed up to be a boxer. There were about eight male students total who participated. My match was set up for the third week in the fall. I started training. I ran two miles every day. I was getting in shape to box the student. The other student smoked cigarettes in the bathroom and outside of school. The student body placed a bet on the other student.

The fight had a total of three rounds. The basketball coach was the referee. I was moving around so I wouldn't get hit. I was throwing jabs, not hard enough to hurt him, but he wanted to hurt me. He hit me so hard on the right side that it temporarily knocked the wind out of me. I realized that I needed to hit him as hard as he wanted to hit me. I hit him with some hard punches, he fell over, and the coach called the fight. I won.

Jesus and His Angels Watch Over All of Us

I worked in the school cafeteria, and this helped me to be able to afford lunch. I had to wash the pots and pans and set the food for the student body.

At our house, there was a lot of wallpaper. My father had my siblings, and 1 scrub the wallpaper off. We then painted the house. My father bought oil-based paint, so we had to use turpentine to thin the paint. These skills helped me to work on my house tater.

Spring of 1963, 1 wanted to go to prom, but I did not have money for a tux. My mother said she would help me. I had enough money to rent the shoes and tux and afford dinner for my date. The tux I rented was black; the shirt was white and black with ruffles down the shirt and black buttons. My date had a beautiful pink and yellow dress with black patent leather shoes. 1 gave her a carnation. My date was a  neighbor down the street. My car was no longer working, so

I had an older friend who graduated two years early take me and my date to the prom. Prom was great, and my date and I enjoyed dinner afterward.

My classmates said the following about me. A smile shoots out with all molars, showing all his teeth. Finas is up to something. Finas is a friend indeed to all in need. Sport he played was basketball.

Spring of 1963, I graduated.

After graduation, I found a job that paid $1.25 an hour. It was a manufacturing job. My mother helped me sign my second car. It was a 1959 Chevy Biscayne. I paid about $250 for the car. It was a four-door stick shift, six-cylinder. I worked from 3 pm until midnight Monday through Friday, and some Saturdays were time and a half. My mother taught me how to cook, and I would bring my lunch. My friends helped teach me how to work on my car. My friend had a garage, and his dad would let us use the garage to practice fixing our cars.

Summer of 1963, my car broke down. The motor went out. I was going to buy a new motor, but my dad's friend said we should go to the junkyard because we could save money. I was able to find a motor for $50. I then had to replace spark plugs, distributor cap, clutch, pressure plate, carburetor, and hoist. It took about a week for us to get the car running. We did not save any money.

I learned how to put a jack stand under a car. They were one-legged jacks that people would use to prop up their cars to work underneath them. The news outlets were telling people not to use these jacks to prop their cars and work underneath them because the jack was not strong enough and the car could fall on them. There were deaths reported. One day my dad was working on his car, and he had the car jacked up with a one-legged jack.

The tire was removed. I told him he needed something else besides the one-legged jack to help him support the car. He told me no. I found a couple of cement blocks to help support the vehicle. After a while, the one-legged jack slipped, and the car fell, but he was fine because the blocks kept the car from crushing him. He got up, dusted himself off, and went into the house. He did not come out of the house the rest of that evening. I finished working on the car. I took off the starter and put the new starter on.

I taught my aunt how to drive a stick shift. She later burned up the clutch in the car and bought a new automatic Pontiac. I also taught a young lady how to change the oil in her car. The materials needed to change your car's oil are a hydraulic jack, two jack stands, an oil pan, a filter wrench, oil, a crescent wrench, and an oil spout. Raise your car, take the oil cap off the engine, and put jack stands under the car's frame.

As the oil drains, you take the filter wrench and take the oil filter off. Now replace the old oil filter with a new one. Put the nut in the hole and tighten the nut on the oil pan. Take the oil spout and put the oil into the engine. Screw the engine cap back on the oil. The engine cap should be the last thing you put back on. Take your jack stand out from under the car and oil pan from under the car. Find a place to get rid of your old oil. Make sure to put all your tools back.

I bought a new washer machine for my mother. We went to the furniture store, and it cost around twenty dollars to get the washer machine hooked up. Love for my mother. I started paying my mom $30 a month for rent to help her out—love and Respect for my mother.

In the fall of 1963, I worked a Saturday job cleaning buildings. A couple of the employees there invited me out to drink with them. We finished work at 9 pm. They told me to follow them in my car. We went to a farm, and they provided me with beer. Every time I finished a bottle of beer,, they ensured my hand was not empty. I had drinks back to back- until about

11 pm. I was ready to go home. On my way home, I stopped and got a shake, cheeseburger, and fries. I was about five miles from home, and I began to feel sick. Once I finally got home, I used the bathroom. My mother called and asked if that was me coming into the house. My parent's bedroom was right underneath the stairs. Once I got to my room, I removed my clothes and lay down. The bedroom began to spin. I jumped up to the bathroom and threw up in the toilet. Next 18 days my mother came to my room, brought a cold towel, placed it on my head, and said, "Uh huh." I knew better.

Chapter 5

In January of 1964, I was awarded a Letter of Appreciation for finding a lost diamond ring in my department at work. On Friday afternoon, January 10, 1964, Finas Black found a 14 Ksrst Keepsake diamond ring. Immediately upon finding the ring, he gave it to his supervisor. The supervisor held onto the ring until Monday, January 13, 1g54_ He was sure the ring belonged to an employee in the department. The female employee called the supervisor Friday night to notify him that she had lost the ring. The ring was returned to the employee on Monday, January 13th, 1964. Mr. Black was commended for his honesty. In the spring of 1964, I went on vacation for a week in Minnesota. I had a week off.

It was about 400 miles from Omaha. It took about six and a half hours. The interstate was not yet completed. I made sure that when I got to MN, at my cousin's house, I called my mother to let her know I made it safely. I stayed at my cousin's house for about five days; Minnesota has a lot of beautiful lakes; ln the summer of 1964, my sister introduced me to a lovely young lady.

We became really good friends. We went on dates to the movies and out to eat. We always dressed our best. Me in a suit and tie and her a beautiful dress. We drove around different small towns, brought a blanket, and sometimes had picnics. That year I had Thanksgiving with her family. This beautiful lady eventually became my wife. One day I was headed to the store with my girlfriend, and I saw my friend.

He asked if he could join us, and I said yes. We got to the store, and my girlfriend and friend stayed in the car. When we returned to the car, my girlfriend said he tried to talk to me. He says she is a liar. I told him I believed her and I didn't believe you. Next time you ask me for a ride, and I'm with my girlfriend, I will not give you a ride. Is this a friend or not? In the late fall of 1964, my 1959 Chevy started acting up. It would; not begin in the morning; it had to be jump-started every morning. I brought an extra battery to start it up. It still did not start without a jump; I tried the generator. It was working; battery cables were tighter, and the car would run all day when I would turn it off and on.

So I got a new car, a 1965 Chevrolet Cheval Malibu. I asked my dad if he would sign for the brand-new car. He said yes. I went to the credit union at my job they said yes. But the loan was $1.900.00 the car was $2.300.00. I had the car ordered the last week in November 1964. I put down

$100.The car was delivered to the dealership two weeks before Christmas. I need three hundred dollars. Where was I going for three dollars? Jesus Christ answered my prayer; on Christmas Eve morning, the dealership called and said they could take my car for three hundred dollars as a trade-in. We did the paperwork on the new car.

I gave them the car title, the check, and my keys to the 1959 Chevrolet, and they gave me the keys to the brand-new car. That was my Christmas present to me. I tested-drove the car on the highway and around the city before I went home to my parent's house. I show everybody at my parents' house. I went to my lady friend's parent's home and showed them the new car. My lady friend and I went and showed all her people the new vehicle; then we went back to her parent's home for dinner.

So I started having a headache so bad that my head was & just pounding; every kind of headache medicine did not work for me. I went to the doctor; he thought I had an Orlan problem. The doctor put me in the hospital and ran various tests, and I had no brain problem. So the doctor entered my room and said nothing was wrong with my brain. Then the doctor asked me what I was doing to make my head hurt like that. I told them I was working two jobs, about 14 hours a day. He asked me why. I said I needed money to pay the tax and get the car license. The doctor said to call the tax people and ask if you could pay them, and they said yes. I quit the part-time job; I got the license for the car. I told myself I wouldn't have a headache like that anymore. So as of today j I have no more headaches no more.

In the Spring of 1965:

I decided to go to Denver, Colorado, which is about 540 miles, about 1O hours drive time, and the interstate was not completed yet. I talk to a lot of people about Denver, Colo. My mother said if you wanted to do that, you must get the car out of your daddy's name. I said I would do that. Then I talked to one of my coworkers on the job. He said I would like to buy the car. Since it was a brand new Chevrolet in 1965, and he came to get the transfer title, the credit union transferred my name and Daddy's name off the title. They took our name off the payment plan and put the coworker's name on it and the title. I was free of the car payment.

Chapter 6

In the winter of 1965, I worked two jobs, one in the morning and one in the evening. When I went to file my income tax and found out that I owed about 300.00 dollars; at the time, I did not have the money to pay the tax. My car license had no money; I owed about 100.00 dollars on the license. So I started having a bad headache, so my head was pounding. Every kind of headache medicine did not work for me. I went to the doctor, who thought I had a brain problem. The doctor put me in the hospital and ran various tests, and I had no brain problem.

So the doctor came into my room and said nothing was wrong with your brain. Then the doctor asked me what I was doing to make my head hurt like that. I told them I was working two jobs, about 14 hours a day. He asked me why. I said I needed money to pay the tax and get the car license. The doctor said to call the tax people and ask if you could make payments to them, and they said yes. I quit the part-time job, and I got the license for the car.

I told myself that I wouldn't have a headache like that anymore. So as of today, I do not have any headaches.

In the Spring of 1965:

I decided to go to Denver, Colo., which is about 540 miles, about 10 hours' drive time, the interstate was not completed yet. I talk to a lot of people about Denver, Colo.

My mother said if you wanted to do that, you must get the car out of your daddy's name.

I said I would do that. Then I talked to one of my coworkers on the job. He said I would like to buy the car. Since it was a brand new Chevrolet in 1965, he came to get the transfer title.

The credit union transferred my name and Daddy's name off the title. They took our name off the payment plan and put the coworker's name on it and the title. I was free of the car payment.

The coworker said that he has a 1955 Chevrolet Bel Air that is paid off, and he would trade his car and two hundred dollars, then will have money to go to Denver, Colo. I said yes. The coworker said the 1955 Chevrolet Bel Air is a manual shift on the floor three-speed v8; he said his Chevrolet would make it to Denver, Colo. The coworker said I had an oil change and put in a spark plug and filter. The coworker said I have good tires on the Chevrolet. The coworker gave me the title, which he and the car keys signed.

Chapter 7

In the early Summer of 1965:

I left Omaha, Ne, at about 6:00 am, headed toward Denver, Colo. I said goodbye the day before. But I said I would be real soon. The highway speed was about 75 miles an hour. The journey was about 540 miles from Omaha, Ne. At that time of year, there were not a lot of cars on the road. I was driving about 80 miles per hour. I noticed in my rear mirror that a car was approaching me quickly. So I slowed to 75 per hour; I thought it was the police. But it was not the police.

It was a light blue Pontiac, two doors hard top. The car passed me like I was not moving. In a few minutes, I couldn't see the car. I drove about three hundred miles about until 10:00 am. I stop in a small town and fill the car with gas. I called my mother on the pay phone and told her I was fine. The car was running well. I called my lady friend to talk to her for a short time. I got to Denver, Colo., at about 3:00 pm. Omaha, Ne, we are about one hour ahead of Denver, Colo.

I went to the lady's house my mother's friend knew and knocked on the door. The renter lady came to the door. I let her know who I was; she was glad I made it to her home. We talked a little; then she took me to see the room. So I like the room, it has a bed and a chest drawer. She showed me the bathroom. The landlord lady told me the rent was $15.00 weekly; I said ok. I paid her two weeks of rent; she showed me I had a refrigerator space. I asked her how much it would cost to call my mother and lady friend.

She said it was free this time. She said you would be charged $5.00 monthly; I said ok. The landlord said here is your mother and lady friend's phone number. I called my mother and told her I had made it to Denver. Colo. and gave her the phone number. Then I called my lady friend and let her know I had made it to Denver, Colo. I gave the telephone number to her. About the middle part of June 1965, I found two jobs. I found a movie theater job as a janitor. The second job was with a maintenance company. I received a letter from The White House in Washington on August 3, 1965.

The letter said:

Dear Fellow Worker:

Many people in government and industry, too. For that matter began in jobs similar to yours. They gained skill and confidence and then went on to more education and better jobs. They are proud of their beginnings and government positions today, and I am proud to welcome you into the ranks of government workers. I hope this will not be your last work experience with the government.

Sincerely,

The President of the United States

In August 1965

My lady friend and my sister with her friend came and visited me in Denver, Colo. They came on the bus, and I picked them up from the bus station. It was a Friday evening; I told my landlord lady that lady friend and my sister with her friend came to visit me. The landlord lady asked where they would stay. I said to the hotel. The landlord lady said no, they can stay with us in my house. They can stay in your room, and you sleep on the sofa; I said that would be good. Thank you. So we went out on the front porch to discuss what we could do for Saturday.

I called my male friend up, and he had a lady friend. We talked about a picnic up on a small mountain in a park. On Saturday morning, we brought the chicken that was already cooked, mashed potatoes and gravy, corn on the cob, a bottle of soda pop and ice, cups, forks, spoons, and plates. I and my lady friend and my sister rode in the front seat. My male friend, his lady friend, and my sister's girlfriend rode in the back seat. Everything was nice at the picnic. We all went for a walk up the small mountain to look over the city. Then we started down the small mountain. My male friend said let's run down the mountain, but my lady friend said no. He said when you jump over a bush, keep your feet turned toward you.

On my first jump, I forgot what he said just that quickly, so I failed down the mountain face first. I slipped down on my chest, about fifteen feet. My lady friend and my sister helped me get up. My chest hurt real badly, so they put me in the car, in the back seat, and my lady friend held my head in her lap. My sister was in the back seat. My male friend drove quickly to the hospital; my male friend's lady was upfront with my sister's girlfriend in the front.

The police stopped us to find out why we were going so fast; my friend said the guy in the back had failed down a mountain, so the police escorted us to the hospital. We went to the hospital; they got me a wheelchair to push me inside the examination room and check me in. I was able to see the doctor in about ten minutes.

The doctor said there were no broken ribs or heart or stomach problems. They just bruised ribs; they wrapped my chest with ace bandages and gave me a couple of pain pills.

They told me not to do anything for a couple of days. My male friend drove him and his lady friend back to their place. My lady friend, sister, and girlfriend did not know how to go.

I drove back to the rental home with my lady friend, sister, and girlfriend. It was getting close to the evening, and we all watched the television until bedtime. The next day I took my lady friend, sister, and girlfriend back to the bus station. At about 7:30 am so they could return to Omaha, Ne., we said goodbye until next time.

In the first part of September 1965:

I applied for a job with the railroad company; they said they would let me in about two weeks. I put a wedding ring in the layaway for my lady friend. The army sent a draft notice to report back to Omaha, Ne., to the draft board in the last of Sept. in 1965. I called the draft board and asked if I could be transferred to the Denver, Colo., draft board. I said that I live in Denver, Colo., and they said yes, I could do that. The Denver, Colo, draft board sent me a notice saying it would be a while before I was drafted.

In September, I went to a bar with a friend to buy a drink. When we walked into the bar,, a World Champion Boxer was drinking. I asked him if I could shake his hand because I was a fan of his, and he said yes. I ordered a cherry cola, we talked, and he was down because of the boxing match he had lost. I put my fist on the bar beside his hand, and his hand was twice as big as mine. I thank him for letting me talk to him. In about the first week of October 1965, I put a wedding ring in the layaway for my lady friend and was hired by the railroad company. I was looking for a job as a porter.

But got hired as a brakeman and switchman on the freight train. I was the first black man hired in 1965 as a brakeman and switchman. Part of the job was learning to work 14 days without pay. I had to read the regulations and rules and learn them. Work every shift on nights and days for 14 days. Learn how to sign the engineer to stop and go back, slow down, with a towel or piece of paper for the day, and time at night, we had to use a lantern.

My 14 days and nights came so I could get paid. I worked on an extra Board at different times each day. The money was good. I got the ring out of the layaway by 10-4-1965. My lady friend called me one day and said she was having a baby. In September 1965 asked her if she would marry me, and she said yes. When I got to Omaha, I made it official, and she said I would be thrilled to be Mrs. Black. I came home on Nov 1, 1965. I went to my parent's house and told them the good news of my getting married and that they would be grandparents.

Also, in October 1965, the draft board said I had to report to the army on November 5, 1965. I was able to work and received one paid check. Then I had to ask my supervisor to get off on Nov 1, 1965, and asked him if I would have a job when I got out of the army, and he said yes. I told the rent lady that I was going home to my parents' house. I was leaving to go back to Omaha, and stopped for gas; I called the rent lady to let her know that the car was running well. I went to my lady friend's parent's house, and gave her a ring. I said we would get married in February 1966.

I called the landlord lady in Denver and told her I was home and that my lady friend and I are getting married and having a baby. My lady friend stayed with me and my parent's house until I went to the service. On the 3rd of November, I asked my dad if I could park my car in his garage until I got out, and he said yes. I took my lady friend home to her parent's house and said our goodbyes. My plane had five passengers and Stewarts and two pilots. I took a cab to the airport and got there at 5:30 am. We had to be in Denver at 8:00 am. It was 2 hours behind the Omaha time zone. We had to wait at the airport until the recruits came. There were a lot of guys being drafted into the US Army.

Chapter 8

November 1965:

At the start of my life in the service, there were about 30 of us that were being drafted into the service. We signed into the service, and some went into different branches of the service, Air Force, Marines, Navy, and US Army. The doctor at the recruitment station gave us a quick examination of our eyes, ears, throat, heart, and feet, and we had to bend over, and the doctor put his finger in our butt holes to check for colon cancer. I passed the examination and was officially in the service. After I passed the examination, I got our identification number. The US indicated was for the men who got drafted, and the RA was for the men who volunteered to go into the different branches of services.

I became a Soldier. Now they started to hand out uniforms for the different branches of service. Since I was drafted into the Army, I got green fatigue. Two caps, five pairs of socks, five pairs of green pants, five shirts, five pairs of undershirts, one green jacket, and 2 pairs of black boat dress shoes. I also received two pairs of brown pants, shirts, a trench coat, and a hat. These were our travel clothes by plane, taxi, or bus. The green clothes were used for work and inspection.

We went out to get our orders. The recruiter put me on a bus to a holding area in Fort Louisiana. I got on the airplane with orders, flew into town, and got on a bus and took me to the Fort. I was down there waiting for additional orders to go to another fort for basic training. In the meantime, I learned how to exercise and make up a bunk bed where you could bounce a quarter off it. Two weeks later, the orders finally came down for me to go to Fort Colorado.

I packed my things and took the bus to Colorado, where I started basic training the next day. Breakfast was at Bam, lunch at noon, and dinner at 4:30 pm. The basic training was like training for basketball and football teams but only harder. We learned to walk in groups, learn to stand attention, which means no looking, eyes straight ahead, and don't slouch, don't move the head to watch the set. You had to make your bed in the morning, have no facial hair, get a haircut every week, and learn how to march, walk and hike a two-mile hike with a backpack every day.

I was looking around while standing in attention, and the sergeant would catch me looking and said Black give me

20 pushups. I was out of step marching, and the sergeant would catch me out of step and say Black give me 30 pushups. In one week, I did so many pushups I thought my name was Finas Pushup Black. I learned how to be a soldier that night. Basic training was for about four weeks, from mid-November to mid-December. We were able to leave for four days to go back home. When I got home to my parent's house, I called my lady friend to let her know I was home for a visit. I went into my parents' garage to get my car out.

When I opened the garage door, the lock was broken. We were able to leave for four days to go back home. When I got home to my parent's house, I called my lady friend to let her know I was home for a visit. I went into my parents' garage to get my car out. When I opened the garage door, the lock was broken. My car tires were gone, my car was on blocks, the battery was gone, and the carburetor was gone. The latch on the outside door was broken. My mother said she checked the door a week ago, and it was fine. I called my lady friend to let her know what had happened and walked 11 blocks to her house.

Later the next day, I called the salvage yard, and they came by and picked up the 1955 Chevy. While in the service, we could not have a car on the base until after the basic training and AIT training was over, then we could have a car on the base. When I went into the service, I weighed 170 pounds; in December 1965, I weighed 200 pounds. A lot of exercise caused me to gain weight and eat a lot of food. I finished the year of 1965 in the service for the holidays, Christmas, New Years away from family, but I called everyone to wish them Merry Christmas and Happy New Year. I started advanced training in the last week of December 1965 and finished the third week in January 1966. In January 1966, I went out to celebrate with a couple of friends after the AIT training was over.

They lived off the post with their girlfriend and wife. They were older guys than me, so I asked them to buy some whiskey and gave them the money. We drank and talked until about 11:00 pm; I had to catch the bus back to the Fort. They showed me where to catch the bus back to the Fort. The bus driver checked our ID to ensure we were soldiers returning to the base. The bus stopped at the gate going into the fort, and an MP came on the bus and, checked our ID, then let us go into the fort. My stop was the second from the last stop. I missed my stop because I went to sleep, and the bus driver woke me up at the end of the line and he said I had to get off the bus.

I said I had money to pay for the ride back to my stop, but he made me get off the bus, and I was about 2 % miles from my stop. It was black and dark outside, so I ran the 2 % miles back to the area I was supposed to be. I looked for a car and found a 1959 Chevrolet Impala for about three hundred dollars. With about 100,000 miles. Two doors hardtop 185 horsepower 283 VB, radio. Heat, power steering, dual exhaust, and automatic transmission. I change the oil and filter, I change the air filter, check the tires are in good shape, I check the antifreeze, and it looks new.

Every time you leave the post, you have to get an order, like going on vacation; I asked the First sergeant if I could go on leave to get married; my lady friend was having a baby, I needed about a week, and he said that would be good. The first sergeant gave the clerk an order to type up my paperwork. I drove the car to Omaha, Ne., about 500 miles or more from the fort. In the first week in Feb. 1966, about 8 hours drive.

Chapter 9

In February 1966:

My marriage adventure In my life. I got married on February 4, 1966, my lady friend, her mother, and sister were there, and my mother was there. I had the rings for me and my lady friend. We got married In front of the Judge and two witnesses there. I kissed my wife, and she was very happy. I took my wife, my mother, my mother In law, and my sister In law to lunch. I became a husband, a son In law, a brother-in-law, and an uncle.

My beautiful wife stayed with me at my parents' house. About four days ago, my wife was about seven months pregnant. Then I had to go back to service. I called my wife and mother to let them know I had returned to the fort. My pay was about $ 70.00 monthly, so I paid my wife for part of my money. The service gave her more money too.

In March 1966:

Everything was going well.

In April 1966:

In April 1966, I was shooting at a target at the rifle range. When my sergeant came up to me, said Black. Your wife Is about to die. Do you want to go home and see her? Yes, I said yes, and he said ok, let's get back to the barracks. So you can shower and change clothes In your blue-green dress. There Is a plane going to the air force base close to Omaha, Ne. I missed the airplane, so I went back to the barracks. I called my mother to ask her to send me about twenty dollars to catch a bus, airplane, and taxi.

It took her about two hours to send the money. I had to catch a bus going to Denver, Colo. it took about 2 hours for the bus to get to Denver, Colo. it was about 79 miles. Then it was about 40 miles to the airport from the bus station. When I got to the airport, I was about 10 minutes late, and the plane had taken off going to Omaha, Ne. I had to wait about 4 hours. Military personnel did not have to pay to fly home; we were on standby. See if there was any space on the flight. I was the last one to get on the plane in first class. I arrived in Omaha, Ne. about two hours later. I got a taxi driver trying to take me the long way around to my parent house. I said no, I live here.

The taxi driver went the way I told him to go. I took my duffer bags out of the taxi, paid him, and took them into the house. I asked my dad to take me to the hospital. He said no, I can't take you because I took my medicine, which makes me drowsy. You drive the car with the keys on the chest. My daddy owns a 1959 Ford 4 doors car; I left my parents' house to head for the hospital. It was about 8 miles away. This was a Friday night; it started to rain.

I was not thinking very well. I had my mind on my wife as she was about to die. I applied the brake, but the car slid into the last car, but the other car and driver got out of the way. I bent the fender, not the headlight, on the right side of my daddy's car, and the fender was rubbing against the tire. The police came and gave me a ticket running in the back of the car. I called my brother to see if he had ten dollars for the tow truck driver to bring the car back to the house. He said yes. I had my brother wake up my dad to tell him I had an accident with his car. My daddy said I was all right, and my brother said yes.

I went around to my uncle and aunt's house to see if they were home, but they were gone. I tried to stop the bus that was going my way, but it was out of service. The hospital that I had to go to was about 5 miles away. So I started to walk and run. I got about two and a half miles done in about a half hours. I saw the hospital light about two and a half miles away. It was set on a hill. I started to run some more;

my dress green wool suit was soaked wet from the rain. I kept running and walking. I make it in about 45 minutes.

I said hello to my mother and hugged her, I said hello to my mother In law and hugged her, and I said hello to my sister In law and hugged her too. My mother and my mother In law showed me the baby girl and asked what the baby's name was. I said I would name the baby girl after I saw my wife. When I went to my wife, I said it was not my wife, and they said she was. She was all swollen up. Feet, hands, and the rest of her body. She had a disease called toxemia pregnancy. When I went back to the waiting area. My mother In law and my sister In law wanted me to name the baby. I said no. I said I would name the baby when my wife got better or died. I said a prayer for her to get better, the prayer was the Our Father, and I asked Jesus to give me strength too.

The doctor said she had 72 hours to make it. She was In a coma. She had done at least nineteen hours so far. I was sitting In a chair next to the bed In a corner. The doctor said to wake him up to send him out of the room. The nurse said he had come a long way from the service In Colorado to be here with his wife. He was exhausted. So the doctor and the nurses turned her over on her stomach and gave her a shot In her hip; she screamed In pain and was In a coma. The needle was about nine Inches long. I got up after the doctor and nurses left the room. I called my first sergeant to tell him I needed more time In Omaha, NE. My wife was still in a coma, but the doctor said she would be waiting very soon. The sergeant asked me how much time I needed; I said about a week; he said if I needed more time, let him know. He said he would have the clerk type it up and send it to me by western union.

My wife woke up about three days later. It took about two more days for her to see the baby. My wife and I named the baby L. Black. I went to my parent's house a couple of days early after leaving the hospital to get my daddy's car back together. I had to call my dad's friend and ask him to help me fix my daddy's car, which had a broken headlight and bumper o. So my dad's friend and I went to the salvage yard, found all the parts, and put them back in the car. My aunt, who I have taught me how to drive a stick shift, took me out for my 21st birthday to a nightclub. My birthday was In early April.

About two days later, my wife left the hospital, and I brought her home to her parent's house. I was able to stay at home with her for about three days. Then I have to go back to the service. I took a plane back to Denver, Colorado, and a bus to the fort. In the spring of 1966: I became a daddy In 1966, and my wife became a mother before Mother's Day. But she had to stay In Omaha, Ne., for about four to six weeks. Before she and the baby come to the fort. I must find a home before she and the baby come to the town outside the fort. I found a place to live in a two-bedroom house behind the Landlord's house. It was a furnished house with two bedrooms, a kitchen, a living, a bathroom, and a park in the backyard. I waited for an order to work that day in the last week of May. The sergeant said the clerk was going home for about a month.

The sergeant asked if anyone knew how to type on a typewriter. After saying I could do it three times, he asked, "Can you type?" I said, "Yes." He said, "Where did you learn to type?" I said, "In high school." I typed up a beautiful letter for him. He said he would let me know. I told the sergeant I would be gone for a few days early Friday morning. Later that evening, I left to go to Omaha, Nebraska. Before I left Omaha, Nebraska, my mother In-law got the baby a basket, blanket, clothes, baby bottles, and a blanket for our bed. My mother gave me some money for gas and food. My family and I left Omaha, Nebraska, about Sam Sunday morning. Everything was going great until about 4 pm, the fan belt broke and broke the blade on the fan.

The fan blade broke part of the alternator. The auto part store was closed on Sunday evening, about 80 miles from the base. I called the first sergeant, and we would be late on Monday morning. There were no hotels ln the area, so my family and I went to the truck stop to eat. Then we returned to the car; we had to spend the night in the car. We had blankets! In Colorado, the nights are cold. The truck driver said to drive my car ln front of his truck. He said you have a lovely family, and he would watch over my family. He said he had a shotgun and slept lightly, and would protect my family. Everything went fine during the night with no problems. We went to the auto store and put the alternator on the car.

I had no more problems with the car. Except for the fan blade, the truck driver knew how to fix the four blades on the car and make it a two-blade by breaking one blade and making it into two blades, and then it worked ok. I stopped at the truck stop to find out what happened to the car. That's when I found out the fan belt and alternator were broken. A truck driver saw that I had the hood up on the car. He asked me If he could help me fix the car. I said, "Yes." He said he had tools to help take the fan belt off. The truck stop had a belt but no alternator. Before we left the truck stop, I thanked the truck driver, shook his hand, said, "God bless you," and thanked Jesus for his help. I drove onto the little town outside of the fort. I took the family to the house went In and changed my clothes into my service uniform.

I went into the fort and reported to the first sergeant. My family and I went to church on Sunday at the fort, the priest, after mass. The priest said, "Can I talk to you for a moment?" I said yes. The priest asked if I was married, and I said yes. The priest then asked me if I was married In the Catholic Church, and I said no. The priest asked if my family would like to be married Into the Catholic Church; I said yes. The priest said you need to have a witness. Then he asked whether you would have the baby baptized. My wife said she would like to be baptized too.

The Priest said how about next Sunday after mass. I asked about the wedding on Saturday, June 11, 1966, at about 2:00 pm. The priest said yes, but you need a witness; I said ok. The Second Wedding in 1966: The only person I saw at the Catholic Church on Sunday was a service officer who helped the priest serve the mass. So I sat down and wrote him a letter. The letter said sir, my name is Finas C. Black; I will be getting married on June 11, 1966, on a Saturday at 2:00 p.m. at the Catholic Church on the post. I like to know if you would be a witness at my wedding.

I am in your battalion, the artillery unit. I live off the post. Here is my landlord's telephone number. Thank You. Finas C. Black Then I send the letter and envelope to the officer. It was about two weeks before the wedding. The officer had his staff officer call me up on Tuesday of the week of the wedding. The landlord came and told me an officer called for me on the phone, a very important call. The officer asked if I was Finas C. Black, and yes, I was him.

The officer said that another officer wanted to come to your wedding. The officer said the main officer wanted to know if you would wear civilian or military clothes. I asked the officer what I should wear; the officer said don't care what you wear to the wedding; it's your wedding. I said I am going to wear civilian clothes to my wedding. On June 11, 1966, my wife and daughter were at the church from about 1:30 pm until the wedding started at 2:00 pm. My wife and I had to remove our wedding rings and let the main witness officer hold the rings.

My wife and I did the whole wedding ceremony all over again. My wife and I put the rings on each other's fingers. The priest said we were husband and wife; you may kiss the bride. The priest and the officer had cake, ice cream, coffee, and Juice for us. The main officer asked me how my family lived on an E-1 pay grade. I have been ln the service for over eight months. I said I didn't know, but it was very hard; the main officer looked at me, smiled, and walked away. When I came back to work on June 13, 1966. The officers and the soldiers were waiting for me. They saluted, shook my hand, and congratulated me for getting married. I thank everyone.

Chapter 10

The promotions, clerk type, and medals ln 1966.

On June 14, 1966, ln the formation, the sergeant was to send all the soldiers to do challenging jobs. Then the sergeant asked me if I wanted to be a clerk ln the office, and I said yes. The sergeant said I would start today; the other clerk would show me what to do ln the office. The other clerk was leaving at the end of the week. On June 15, 1966, I started to work as a clerk to learn the morning report and type up letters for the officer ln charge of the office. On June 18, 1966, a young man came and knocked on the rental door, said he was from a pantry ln the city where I lived, and asked me If I was Finas C. Black; I said yes. The young man said I have a box of food for you and your family.

One bag of apples, one gallon of milk eggs. Three cans of green beans, three cans of corn, cereal, a bag of potatoes, and two packs of meat. The order came down from headquarters, and on June 20, 1966, I was promoted to an E-2 with more money ln my pocket. The order came down from headquarters on July 23, 1966. I was promoted to an E-3 with more money ln my pocket. About four days later, I walked to the main headquarters to take the morning report.

The main officer, a witness at my wedding, was on his staff with his driver. The officer had his driver stop. The officer said good morning, PFC Black. Where you are going, I said, going to the main headquarters. The primary officer asked if I wanted a ride; I said yes, Sir, thank you. When I got ln the car, the main officer asked me how the wife and daughter were doing; I said they were doing very well. When we got to the main headquarters, I got out of the car and said, " Thank you for everything you have done for me and my family; the main officer smiled at me and drove away.

In the 2nd week of September ln 1966:

I went ln front of a review board to get another promotion. The review board asked me about the Job I was during and how to do a morning report. How to type letters up about the service. I answer all their questions. But I had to wait until October 1966 before I could be promoted.

The start of college:

Do you have a dream of going to college after being out of high school for about two years? If yes. September 21, 1966, I want to be an Electronics Engineer. So I want to attend college for about ten months while ln the service. I got permission to go to college after my service work at night. The class I was ln was Electronics Principles. The class was

48

on a Thursday from 6:00 pm to 8:00 pm. The first class was on September 25, 1966, to December 21, 1966. The second class started on January 9, 1967, lt was Tubes and Semiconductor; the class was on Tuesdays from 6:00 pm to 8:00 pm and ended on March 1967. The third class started on June 19, 1967. Freshman English One class started at 6:30 pm and 9:00 pm Monday and Wednesday, ending on July 31, 1967. The class was for three-quarters of an hour.

In October 1966:

I want to further my advancement as an office clerk. So I applied for a transfer of my MOS from artillery to a clerk typer. It was a proverb by my 1st sergeant and officer. But the order came down from our battalion on October 31, 1966; I was promoted to Specialist E-4, another pay grade.

In November of 1966:

The orders came from our headquarters on November 5, 1966; I was a clerk type. The owner of the house I was renting said I had to move in about two weeks. I was lucky to find a house ln another small town closer to the fort ln a short period of time. The house had two beds, a living room, a dining area, a kitchen, and one bath. It had all the furniture ln the house. One of the soldiers that got promoted at the same time I did was an E-4 too. The soldier was moving out, and In about four months, the soldier was getting out of the service.

In November of 1966:

I started attending an Institute school for a typewriting class on the fort. I went to school for about two weeks to learn how to get better at typing. I passed the class on November 16, 1966.

In December of 1966:

In the last week of December, I was issued a rifle to learn how to shoot It. The service put our name on the rifle hander. I learn to shoot, hold the rifle, and march with the rifle. I learned how to take the rifle apart and put it back and how to oil the parts of the rifle.

In January 1967:

Starting with the qualifications of the pistol, on January 18, 1967, I had one day to practice shooting the pistol. It was a 45 cal. I qualified as a sp4 E-4; my score was 340. That made me a sharpshooter. The award for the sharpshooter came out on January 25, 1967. I learned how to shoot, hold a rifle, and march with a rifle. I learned how to take the rifle apart and put it back together, how to all the parts of the rifle. I told my fellow soldiers the night before that I would be an expert rifleman. They laughed and said no way. Early Tuesday morning, I went to the rifle range to qualify. I was one of the guys who qualified early. On Tuesday, January 31, 1967, I became an expert rifleman; I shot down 67 out of 73 targets. I became an expert on the same day. The award for the expert was given to me in February 1967.

In February 1967:

I went to class to learn how to teach the soldiers how to go to Vietnam and fight. The class lasts about four weeks. The officer canceled the class. I was then put on a different board with a few other soldiers. They had too many clerk types.

In March 1967:

Nothing was going ln March's regular work hours. I went to college at night.

In April 1967:

My birthday came and went; I was 22 years old, and I made a unit mall orderly. Also, I was transferred to a new unit on the fort. I was the head of the four clerks. I pass out the assignment to them.

In May 1967:

I went in front of another board review for another up-grade. This time everything went well for me.

In June 1967:

In June 1967, I received an E-5 grade to be a specialist E-5. Black, Finas C. Yes, yes, yes, more money.

In July 1967:

I trained the young clerk to be better at their job and be the best they could be. I went to college at night. I was called a short-timer soldier because I had about three months left ln the service. So I went and started to get the paperwork on getting out of the service and medical records.

In August of 1967:

I bought a brand new Chevrolet Biscayne, which was a full-size car. White on the outside, blue on the Inside Three speed transmission on the column shifted manual. Six cylinder motor, radio, electrical windshield wipers. White walls tires. I got a five-day vacation after I had the car for about a week. My family and I drove to Omaha, Ne. My family and I stay ln Omaha, Ne. After about a day, then we drove to Kansas City, Mo. My family and I are staying with my sister in Kansas City, MO, for a day. I said I like this city; I can make money here.

My wife said she likes the city too.

A few days later, we were on our way back to the fort. My wife and baby saw a sign on the highway saying huge hamburgers. I asked my wife if she wanted a hamburger, and she said yes. We went to a place that sold huge hamburgers. We went into the restaurant, and the owner had us sit down at a table in the middle. The owner had a high chair for the baby. I ordered a huge cheese hamburger with fries. My wife ordered a hamburger.

Well done. The owner said only can cook one at a time. The owner brought the cheese hamburger out of the kitchen on a full-size plate when the cheese hamburger was cooked. The huge cheese hamburger was about 12 Inches big, about a half pound of meat. I told the owner not to cook the other hamburger; we would eat this and be full. I cut the hamburger for me and the wife. My wife orders a root beer float and a strawberry shake. The owner brought the root beer float and the shake out to us.

In September 1967:

I was getting ready to get out of the service. I collect all my papers, dental records, medical records, and financial paper.

In October 1967:

I received the award of GOOD CONDUCT MEDAL from the fort.

Award of the Good Conduct Medal:

Announcement is made of the following, Award for exemplary behavior, efficiency, and fidelity for the period indicated.

BLACK, FINAS C. Sp 5 E-5 from November 1965 to November 1967.

Chapter 11

In November 1967

Finas C. Black IS GOING BACK TO BE A CIVIL-IAN AGAIN. I was HONORABLE DISCHARGE from the service.

I received my last pay from the service, 21 days of vacation plus my salary.

I left the fort at about 3:00 pm with my family and headed to Omaha, Ne. My wife and the baby were ready to return to Omaha, Ne. We stayed overnight ln a small town ln Nebraska. My family and I got to Omaha, NE, the next day. Everybody was glad to see us. I stayed ln Omaha for NE about two weeks. I went to Kansas City, Mo.to get started back work for the railroad. I asked to have my place of employment transferred from Denver, Colo, to Kansas City, Mo. I left my family behind until I found a place to live. I will stay with my sister for about two weeks.

I found a two-bedroom house for rent, and I put a deposit on it; one week later, I went back to Omaha, Ne.to pick up my family. My mother gave me a sofa and my bed and my chest. My mother ln law gave my daughter a crib. Some more clothes, my wife's clothes. I brought a stove and refrigerator at a discount price. I rented a trailer to put the stuff in when I got to Kansas City, Mo. A neighbor helped me put the stove and the refrigerator ln the house. I returned the trailer to the company I rented from, a nationwide company.

In December 1967:

I was glad to be out of the service. I work at the railroad; getting used to life outside of the service took a while: my first Christmas and New Year from the service.

In the summer of 1968:

My wife's father had died ln Omaha, Ne, by accident. The body was shipped to East St. Louis, Illinois. My father's relative wanted him to be buried ln East St. Louis, Illinois. When we would go to Omaha, Ne, my wife and I would see her father.

In August of 1968:

JESUS GIVES YOU EXTRA STRENGTH WHEN YOU NEED IT THE MOST. The family of my wife's father called my wife to let her know what day the funeral was to be. It was set for a Saturday in the second-week ln of August 1968. I asked my sister, who stays ln Kansas City, Mo. Would she take care of the baby for me on Saturday and part of Sunday? She said yes. My wife and I left at about 7:00 am Saturday, my wife and I arrived In East St. Louis, Illinois, at about 10:30 am, and the funeral started at about 11:45 am. My grandfather lives about 1OO feats from the church where the funeral was to be.

My wife and I went to say hello to him and his wife. My wife and I visited the church to review her father's body. Looking down at her father's face, she passed out In my arms. I pick her up and carry them to my grandfather's house. My grandfather helped me to put her on the bed. My grandfather told me to lie down beside my wife and rest.

My grandfather and his wife put a cold towel on my wife's head. My wife woke up and asked for a glass of water. I returned to the church to find out why my wife passed out. The embalming fluid leaked out of her father's head onto the pillow. I returned to my grandfather's house for about 3 hours. Before I got started to go back to Kansas City, MO. I gave my grandfather a great big hug and his wife a hug, too; I thanked them for everything. My wife hugged my grandfather, too, and his wife. My wife and I said goodbye and left, returning to Kansas City, Mo.

In September of 1968:

The first week ln September 1968, I enrolled ln, a machine training ln computer programming class. The school lasts for a month. The school sent me a letter on the last day of September 1968. The letter said:

Dear Mr. Black:

We are pleased to send your diploma showing that you have completed the course ln computer programming at our training center. It was a pleasure to have You ln class.

In October of 1968:

The landlord gave me a letter saying the rent was going up to about 50.00 dollars per month. I told the landlord that I couldn't afford the new rent. The landlord said that I had to move ln one month. About two weeks later, I found a cheap house to live ln. My wife and I and the baby moved out the last week ln October of 1968. Jesus and His Angels Watch over All of Us 35 My wife told me she was about six weeks pregnant.

In November of 1968:

My wife and I had everything she and I had, the stove and the refrigerator. After my wife and I moved ln. I asked the new landlord if he would buy the paint for the kitche and the living room. I would paint the kitchen and living room for him. The landlord said yes, and the landlord brought the paint roller. Brushes. The landlord brought latex paint. I did the work of painting the kitchen and living; I did a great Job. The Landlord said that the kitchen and living room looked very nice. The kitchen and living room are all so swell and very good.

In December of 1968:

Last two weeks ln December of 1968, I put ln my letter saying I would quit the railroad.

In January of 1969:

I started a new Job ln a manufacturing building ln Kansas City, Mo. I was a machine part Inspector, with less money, less stress, easy Job.

In February of 1969:

I started to hear noise ln the house; someone or thing was running up and down the basement stairs. When I went to check, I couldn't find anything.

In March of 1969:

I found out that there were rats In the house. I found the drops from the rats on the stairs and set traps in the basement and on the stairs. I caught two rats In the traps, but the rats were very smart. They spread death on the traps and would not eat any more food from the traps. I brought rat poison, which slowed them down for a white. The rats were In the backyard, with holes all over the place. They didn't try to bite us. But it was hard to sleep at night. I woke up one morning to find out I had three marks on my left arm, so I went to the emergency room.

The doctor said it was a spider bite. I was fortunate that the marks were going down my arm Instead of going up my arm. If the mark were going up, that would go to my heart. The doctor gave me an antibody shot In my arm. I asked the doctor where the spider would be hiding, and the doctor said under the bed, so when I returned to the house, I raised the mattress, and there it was. I killed the spider.

In April of 1969:

My birthday was very nice. VA approved me for a loan on the house. I went all over the city to a small town looking for a house. The realtor said I was not making enough money to buy a house, even with the money that VA guaranteed. I was making the same money as the rest of the people ln the manufacturer where I work. I kept looking for a house.

In May of 1969, the birth of our son:

Around the middle of the month, my wife was pregnant with our second child, and her water broke loose. So I cleaned up the water and prepared her to leave for the hospital. I was lucky the catholic hospital was about six blocks away. I loaded the wife and baby girl away and went to the hospital. I called the hospital before I left home to tell them that my wife was waiting for her to wait at the hospital.

They were waiting at the emergency room door ln a wheelchair. I had to complete the paperwork before going to the delivery room. The nun asked if she could watch the girl while I went to delivery, and I said yes. They cleaned our son up. Our son weighs about 9lb and 2oz. 23 Inches long.

There was no problem for him, my wife. Everything went well. I went and got the baby girl from the nun, and I said thank you. My wife and I named the son Finas C. Black Jr. I called my wife's mother, and she was delighted; she said she would be ln Kansas City, Mo., the next day. She came by airplane the next day; I picked her up at the airport. I took her to see her daughter and grandson. My wife stayed in the hospital for three days before she could come home. My mother ln law helps out around the house. My mother ln law stayed a week before she left.

In June of 1969:

About the second week in June of 1969, I found a house I could get approved on. I had to wait thirty days to move the house after the closing.

In July of 1969:

About the first week ln July of 1969, my grandfather was sick, so I called him up and asked him how he was doing. My grandfather said that his breath was not very good. Hard to breathe at times. My grandfather said he was taking pills to help his breathing.

My grandfather lives ln a little town outside East St. Louis, lii. Where a packing house was located nearby, they switched a lot of train boxcars there. It had about fifteen train tracks. Sometimes you would stop for about one or two hours and wait on the train to clean. About two weeks later, my cousin called me and let me know that our grandfather died ln his sleep the night before. I called my mother and told her what had happened. The funeral was set up about a week later. My mother later called me to see if I was attending the funeral. I said yes, and she said, okay can I go with you down there? I said yes. She was bringing my baby brother, and they were coming by bus, and I would pick her up and my baby brother at the bus stop on Friday. At about noon, I said yes. Me and my wife, two children, my mother, and baby brother rode to the funeral Saturday morning.

We left Kansas City, Mo., at 6:00 am at 9:30 am. There were train switch boxcars A round ln the packing house. We had about fifteen minutes until the train was through under-loading the boxcars. We were on time before the funeral got started. My uncles, aunts, and cousin are just about of the cousins of my grandfather's great-grandchildren. I and my mother, my wife, my children, and my baby brother went to the grave site with the rest of the family. After the repass was over Me and my wife, my children, my mother, and my brother all left, going back to Kansas City, Mo. My mother and baby brother left Sunday morning afternoon on the bus going to Omaha, Ne. About the last week of July of 1969, they said we could move into the house on August 1, 1969.

Chapter 12

In August of 1969: my wife and I signed the papers to move into the house. We had a moving company to move us on August 1, 1969. The moving company came at about 8:00 am to start moving our furniture. They were through for about two hours. The house that my wife and children were ln was delighted, with no rats. I later met with the rental house owner, and he checked out the house. Which was no problem with the house, but the rats had eaten a hole into the living floor. The house owner said he would take care of the rat's problem. The house we moved into was a three-bed-room, ranch one level, one-car garage, large country kitchen, one bath, living room, basement, fence ln the back yard, and a corner lot.

We had moved up to a great house which was our home. The house had a window air conditioner coming out of the garage wall ln the living room.

I was at the grocery store buying food when a friend I know came up to me and said hello I turned to see who it was, the friend who works at the railroad company where I work. The friend said my name was on the bulletin boards at the railroad company. The bulletin board said that I had a check coming. I need to pick up the check real soon. I said I would get the check as soon as I buy the groceries.

DO YOU BELIEVE IN UNSUSPECTED MONEY?

I believe In unsuspected money was a large sum, from the vacation money I didn't get before I left and the extra work I did. This was a great day. In the middle of the month, my wife and I want to change the living color and paint the ceiling light blue. So I came up with the idea to make stairs In the ceiling. My wife said how do you do that? I said it is very simple, buy the paint and rent a glitter machine. Put the paint on In sections at a time, then put the silver glitter into the machine and crank it up. But first put a plastic cover on the floor. That's what we did. It has a great shiny ceiling and looks like the sky with stairs. My friend and relative like the Idea too.

The last week in August of 1969:

I wanted to detail my 1967 Chevrolet car with stairs on the roof of the car. I and my future brother In law came up with the Idea. To paint my white Chevrolet rooftop with a blue wrinkle paint that makes it look like a vinyl top. I and my brother In law went out and brought the paint, about six cans of spray paint, and water sandpaper to sand the top down, so the paint would stick. Do the paint Job on a sunny day so the paint dries fast. Put a sliver of glitter on the roof a section at a time. The sun would bake ln the paint. Then I put baby moon hubcaps on all four tires. I put a black pinstripe. On the side of the car, on the front hood, and the trunk of the car.

In September of 1969:

I enrolled ln the Electronic Engineering Course. I had to have a Certificate of Eligibility to enroll ln the course. I received the certificate on September 1, 1969. I am working for a manufacturing company. I start the Electronic Engineering Course at the end of the month. I work from 3:30 pm to 12:00 am Monday through Friday. I go to school Monday through Friday, 8:00 am to 2:00 pm, and I am a family man too.

This is the class I took to learn Engineering. The class went from September of 1969 to the last of December of 1969.

Electricity: I make a (C) grade.

Algebra: I make a (C) grade.

Chemistry: I make a (C) grade.

English: I make a (C) grade

Engineering Graphic: I make a (C) grade.

The next set of classes started on January 1970.

In October 1969:

I was going to school, work, enjoying my wife and children, and Sunday church. We drove to Omaha, Ne, a couple of times ln October of 1969. They were glad to see the baby boy. My son was so heavy no one wanted to hold him very long. My wife and I brought a baby stroller just for him.

Chapter 13

In November 1969:

The slap on the face and kick In the butt. And no accident: I went to school and worked every day during the week In November of 1969. The second week In November of 1969, I and a group of employees talked about nothing in the break room. When this other employee called me Finas, I turned toward him and said I would slap that smile off your face. I looked him in the eyes and said when you do that, the next time you go to a baseball game, you will have one hand and one arm and will miss. The employee said what you are talking about. I said my knife will cut off your hand and arm, and you will have one hand and one arm.

The employee said I was playing with you. HAI HAI The employee didn't talk to me anymore or come around me know more. If the employee saw me come, the employee would turn around and go the other direction about the last two weeks of November of 1969. I was still going to school and working every day during the week.

A couple of employees and I were talking In the break room. Another employee worked on the job. He came into the room, pointed toward me, and said he would kick my butt. Because he didn't like me, the cause was too happy. I walked toward him, stopped about two feet away, and said, "When you kick me, ln my butt. You are going to have a wheelchair to come back to work.

The employee said, "What are you talking about?" I said I am going to cut your damn feet and legs off. So that's why you're going to need a wheelchair. I didn't see him in the break room or around the company area.

In December of 1969:

The class of Electronics was over at the end of the month. The next semester I started ln two weeks ln January of 1970. Had my vacation set up for the end of the month ln December 1969, last week ln the month. We and my wife and two children had planned a vacation going to Chicago, lii. to see my wife's mother, sister, niece, and nephew.

My daughter was three years old, and my son was seven months old.

We are packing the clothes that we need for the vacation. We left Kansas City, Mo., on the 23 of December of 1969 at about 8:00 am ln the morning. The trip to St. Louis, Mo. It was a great day, with no snow, wind, and a very sunny day. When you have a big problem and can't figure out what to do, Jesus has the answer and solution to help you. We stopped in St. Louis, Mo., to get gas and use the toilet; we returned to Chicago on the Interstate. I passed a tractor and trailer on the Interstate to Chicago, 11. After I passed the tractor and trailer, I was about three hundred feet ln front of the tractor and trailer. I was talking to my wife. She was changing the baby boy's diaper and putting him back ln the baby basket. My daughter was ln her seat belt. My wife put on her seat belt. But all of a sudden, the steering wheel jerked out of my hand; the car was going to the right into the grass and was heading toward a fence. I turned the steering back to the left and came back up on the Interstate.

The truck driver had stopped, and no other car was coming on the Interstate. The car went across the left lane heading for a small bridge. I turn the steering wheel back to the right. The car came back to the left lane and stopped on the shoulder. I got out of the car to see if there was damage. Yes, there was damage on the right fender. But it didn't stop the car from moving. I waved at the truck driver and gave him the thumbs up. The truck just smiled and shook his head. I returned from the 1967 Chevrolet and put lt gear, and it came up off the shoulder, and we went to Chicago, 11. No one was hurt. When we got to Chicago, li. We told my wife, mother, and sister what happened. They said thank the Lord you were not hurt.

There was a dent on the passenger side of the front fender; my father ln law had a rubber hammer. I knocked out the dent. I called my mother to let her know we had reached Chicago. I told her what happened, and she said thank you, Jesus, that you were safe.

This is the end of book number one. The next book will be on January 1970, out very soon—the end of December 1969.

The employee said, "What are you talking about?" I said I am going to cut your damn feet and legs off. So that's why you're going to need a wheelchair. I didn't see him in the break room or around the company area.

In December of 1969:

The class of Electronics was over at the end of the month. The next semester started ln two weeks ln January of the year 1970. Had my vacation set up for the end of the month ln December 1969, last week ln the month. My wife and two children had planned a vacation to see my wife's mother, sister, niece, and nephew in Chicago, Illinois.

My daughter was three years old, and my son was seven months old.

We are packing the clothes that we need for the vacation. We left Kansas City, Mo., on the 23 of December of 1969 at about 8:00 am In the morning. The trip to St. Louis, Mo. It was a great day, with no snow, no wind, and a very sunny day. When you have a big problem and can't figure out what to do, Jesus has the answer and solution to help you. We stopped in St. Louis, Mo., to get gas and use the toilet; we got back on the Interstate to Chicago, and I passed a tractor and trailer on the Interstate to Chicago. After I passed the tractor and trailer, I was about three hundred feet In front of the tractor and trailer.

I was talking to my wife. She was changing the baby boy's diaper and putting him back In the baby basket. My daughter was In her seat belt. My wife put on her seat belt. But all of a sudden, the steering wheel Jerked out of my hand; the car was going to the right into the grass and was heading toward a fence. I turned the steering back to the left and came back up on the Interstate. The truck driver had stopped, and no other car was coming on the Interstate. The car went across the left lane heading for a small bridge. I turn the steering wheel back to the right. The car came back to the left lane and stopped on the shoulder. I got out of the car to see if there was damage.

Yes, there was damage on the right fender. But it didn't stop the car from moving. I waved at the truck driver and gave him the thumbs up. The truck just smiled and shook his head. I got back in the 1967 Chevrolet and put lt gear, and it came up off the shoulder, and we went to Chicago, 11. No one was hurt. When we got to Chicago, li. We told my wife, mother, and sister what happened. They said thank the Lord you were not hurt.

There was a dent on the passenger side of the front fender; my father ln law had a rubber hammer. I knocked out the dent. I called my mother to let her know we had reached Chicago. I told her what happened, and she said thank you, Jesus, that you were safe.